# Out of the Blue

# Out of the Blue
## Poems: 1982 – 2011
### Selected by James Spence

# Don Gutteridge

*First Edition*

Hidden Brook Press
www.HiddenBrookPress.com
writers@HiddenBrookPress.com

Copyright © 2019 Hidden Brook Press
Copyright © 2019 Don Gutteridge

All rights for poems revert to the author. All rights for book, layout and design remain with Hidden Brook Press. No part of this book may be reproduced except by a reviewer who may quote brief passages in a review. The use of any part of this publication reproduced, transmitted in any form or by any means, electronic, mechanical, photocopied, recorded or otherwise stored in a retrieval system without prior written consent of the publisher is an infringement of the copyright law.

Out of the Blue: Poems: 1982 – 2011
by Don Gutteridge

Cover Design – Sol Terlson Kennedy
Cover Image – Kaiskynet Studios/Shutterstock
Layout and Design – Richard M. Grove
Thanks to Laurie Nicholson for typing the ms
Typeset in Garamond
Printed and bound in Canada
Distributed in USA by Ingram,
    in Canada by Hidden Brook Distribution

**Library and Archives Canada Cataloguing in Publication**

Title: Out of the blue: poems, 1982-2011 / Don Gutteridge ;
    selected by James Spence
Other titles: Poems. Selections.
Names: Gutteridge, Don, 1937- author. | Spence, James, 1994- editor.
Description: First edition.
Identifiers: Canadiana 20190091118 | ISBN 9781927725702 (softcover)
Classification: LCC PS8513.U85 A6 2019 | DDC C811/.54—dc23

Table of Contents

– Psycho-Motoring – *p.2*
– Walking North at Millennium's End – *p.*
– Indian Summer On a Farm Near Preston – *p.5*
– What I Remember – *p.6*
– Skating Out – *p.8*
– Expectation – *p.9*
– The Visit – *p.10*
– Snowbound – *p.12*
– Riel – *p.14*
– Stealing Apples – *p.16*
– Bloodlines or You Never Can Tell – *p.18*
– Possession – *p.19*
– Airborne – *p.20*
– On Watching Tom Play Rugby – *p.21*
– Autumn – *p.22*
– Effie – *p.23*
– The Catch – *p.24*
– Renewal – *p.25*
– Companions – *p.26*
– Heaven – *p.27*
– The Walk – *p.28*
– Every Time it Snows – *p.29*
– Creation – *p.30*
– Labour – *p.31*
– Patsy: The Silence – *p.32*
– Good Measure – *p.34*
– Sketching Anne – *p.36*
– To A Daughter, Writing – *p.37*
– Tom's Song – *p.39*
– Say Uncle – *p.40*
– Home – *p.42*
– Alphabets – *p.44*
– Soliloquy, For Lovers – *p.46*
– The Innocents – *p.49*
– Abelard's Plea – *p.52*
– Afterimage – *p.54*
– Heart: 1944 – *p.55*

- Bones – *p.56*
- Hands – *p.57*
- First Steps – *p.58*
- Routine – *p.59*
- Poet – *p.60*
- Malamute in Snow – *p.61*
- So Big – *p.62*
- God-Spell – *p.63*
- April – *p.64*
- Nouns – *p.65*
- Boyhood – *p.66*
- Immanence – *p.67*
- The Absolute Uncertainty of Being Seven – *p.68*
- Moment – *p.70*
- Walking – *p.72*
- A Word to My Grandsons – *p.74*
- Vivacity – *p.77*
- Wheels – *p.79*
- Necessities – *p.82*
- Where the Voice Abides – *p.86*
- Stories – *p.91*
- Mother – *p.95*
- The Time Between – *p.97*
- Out of the Blue – *p.98*
- The Sands of Canatara – *p.99*
- The Welcoming – *p.100*
- The Word – *p.101*
- It's Hard To Believe – *p.102*
- Me – *p.103*
- Love's Seasons – *p.104*
- The End of Days – *p.105*
- Sin – *p.106*
- Wee – *p.107*
- Music – *p.108*

About the Author – *p. 111*

# Out of the Blue

# Psycho-Motoring
*For James*

At two-and-a-bit the mind
is still a muscle that
warps the world to its
will, a palpable
tongue that has its say
in every ambuscade of
arm-and-leg you utter
against the instigations
of gravity: whole
paragraphs of hilarity
at toe-toppled loco-
motives/dolls decaptitate
hugged prosy again/
free-wheeled vehicles
commandeered in zany
disdain by Mister Toad
on a vivisecting binge
thru hedgerows and
chesterfields (and
bumble-brothers
at odds with the road),
and, oh, the limerick-tick
of your giggle at the logic
of galoshes or polka-
dot beluga-bugs
with plasticine skin ....
Yours is an elfin
bodyspeak,
a whim-poem,
a disquisition
        in delight.

(Yet we would ply you
with the bottle-fed speech
of our own vernacular lives,
and, impenitent, applaud
the first full sentence
of your voice to settle
for something other
than itself.)

## Walking North at Millennium's End

*Eagle Lake, December 1999*

These woods, promising
much, invite me thither:
to a weightless walking
upon snows centuried
serene among spruce and
tamarack stoic in their
infinite repetitions
my feet feel the
all-at-once dither
of directionlessness,
the gravid grip of
rock outcropping,
a polar pull hip-
thick in the thing itself
beckoning forth till I
am become what I am –
unfrocked in the silence
between sun and firmament
where all winds pivot
north

# Indian Summer
# On a Farm Near Preston

*For Margaret and John Barnett*

November breeds
a sun more mellow
and a brown silence
clings to the quiet
fallow of the land,
while hills who have spilled
their seed in a wild September
roll more gently now,
and fields of cornstalk
murmur down the length
of yellowing rows
where the wind has gone
and the orchard trees
lean like old men
dreaming into a brown
silence of sun
that holds the hills
with mellowed eye.

And I see the ruined homestead
where stones have stood
a hundred autumns
and kept them true till spring,
and underneath the quiet earth
I hear November voices
singing of the deep fallow
where all the Indians lie.

# What I Remember

What I remember is the
lake of grandfather's lawn,
the green frenzy, lilac
forests full of poems,
a sun surprised by all this

    AND

what I remember is grandfather's war
the stories he told of it and because
I went there many times after
our death, the gas in my lungs
murderous as McCrae's poem
coming out of him so he could die
you often recited so you could live

    AND

poetry is what I remember
the kind that comes breathless
out of memory not texts:
my mother's Kipling: school-verse
seizing rooms, book-prizes, loves
lost before found, O Gunga
Din was more than a man
you wanted so much more for
me to know in that poem
we could only say it together

## AND

what I remember is you, LaSalle,
who came here without bidding
it says so in this journal,
what-is-more I check it out
and dream you hauling your Griffon
(like a stunned hawk thru
swamps I thought were secret)
to the blue exodus, bootprints
on my own Canatara pointing
northward to Huron, precipice of
memory, the Iroquois don't
know where it begins but
you keep the journal going
past Superior, its blood network,
the Mississippi has no preface
you write it anyway, cram
the last page with your
outrageous scrawl, your lyric/
bombast/plain-word    you
go with them to the edge
walk over and
remember everything

## Skating Out

What are these
miniatures moving
out of the encoving dark,
the marvellously one –
mooned sky   oh
open utterly, they
slide seaward on the
sudden ice/earth but
there is no sea –
sound, no border
line they glide
toward    these wing –
less filigrees
rise wide and
loose oh into the
unutterable moon –
curved dark, the
edge of all ice and
no sound but the
bladed silence
ringing starward
these
child-creatures loom
high and handsome
don't they know
there's no horizon
no words when
stars stymie their
eyes    stretch their
breath    ballooning
they sail the
unuttering oceans
of air
those
miniatures I last
glimpsed skating
the moon's face.

# Expectation
*For Kate, the kids and the one-to-be.*
*(Christmas, 1996)*

In a world where the snows
of Christmas-coming
festoon the death-stares
of innocents estranged
by ethnic gunning and
to-dos over deities,
where politicos dither
like Pontius in his fingerbowl
and the Herods of hate
wither with corrupt touch
olive-grove and inn-yard –
it is hard to hope,
so we don't.

On a street carolled
by children in passionate
play: toboggan-whee!
the boys go tumble –
oh! the girls/skates
keening on poised
blades of
breath
and joy's elixir
at the hither-and-thither
snow-falling as simple
and certain as wishing it
(and closer to home,
the one-to-be:
blood-mangered
coiled as a question
a fiddlehead fist
gesturing to
un-stranger itself
and shake hands
with the startled Magi).

On such an Earth
it is hard not to hope,
so we do.

# The Visit
*For John Barnett*

"I'm old," you say with a wry grin
to explain the misbehaviour
of 87-year-old bones
(the shuffle-step you substitute
for the stride that bore you proud
thru the backwoods of Haliburton
calibrating timber with a bush-
man's affectionate eye)
or the pauses a stiffening brain
stubborns between words once
as seamless as a fisherman's
whopper about the one that got away
or a deerstalker's cracker-
barrel lament.
We are
grateful your smile refutes
all filial pieties,
embraces the brute fact
that the only reason for living
now is living.
Thus, you seem content to sit
and reminisce the random past,
to tell again (in grooves too
habitual to be true) tales
of youthful derring-do
or the forgivable follies of
sibling and neighbour,

to pluck the names of the long dead
from the crammed quarry of memory
like rabbits out of a silk hat,
to part with this weathered album
of photos thumbed to oblivion,
to be generous in judging
the merits of old hurts –
freed at last to speak
of yourself in the third person.

So, we watch with a kind of awe
as your slippered feet deliberate
the steepness of cellar stairs:
you raise your shrunken frame
to the room's height, select
a flawless lozenge of wood
from a cord you might have muscled
square in your prime, and tuck it
into the friendly furnace-flame.
"There," you say, "that'll do for now."

You wave as we wheel away,
happy to be alone, or not:
when the next knock comes,
as it must, you will bide
your breath, make no fuss
whether the visitor be death
or us.

# Snowbound

## I

Outside, the hedge-cedars
double under the weight-
less alabaster vise

Beyond: the roadway reverts
to river, bay, albino sea

In blanched degrees
the eaves succumb
to scroll and filigree
(incorrigible curves)

Inch by hour
the porch is dwarfed

the house surrenders
longitude, flattens
toward sunset or dawn
dark or light, it doesn't
matter when snows come
man-deep and more
than six-feet-by-four.

## 2

But the snow of my childhood ...

tastes like appleflesh
feathers of the snow-goose
we free fall   do a slow
motion crawl in,

and no paths but those I
carve between friendly yards:
a distance quickened
by sled and snowshoe
by the sheer curve of wishing.

Diminished in my two-
globed igloo, albino-blind,
my dream is arctic-tall

or

cast askance the seamless lake
of lawn, field, swamp, the bay's
edge against the westward-climbing blizzard
my dream is eskimo-tiny:

the child's dream of constant snow
the blank obliteration
the zero of a mouth proclaiming "oh!"

## Riel

There is no
eloquence to
blood running
from the mouths
of wounds and
battles lost,
the eyes
of the dead
at Duck Lake
and Batoche are
white stones
darkening
at
the
centre.

I hear
no story
of their suffering
no rhythm
of waters running
blue St. Lawrence
breathing tides
the earth-red
of my own river
blending
to seed of lakes
the world may wait
a hundred suns
to see

When my body
swings like a
dead man's tongue
from the white man's
scaffolding,
will there be
an eloquence
to tell ...

or will this
prairie be
a coffin
for my voice
a dwelling-place
for
        two
        white
                stones?

## Stealing Apples

When we lived
on the fourth line
(it was not a line then
but a road thru greenness
of ragweed and wheat
that ended where our
schoolhouse began)
we would merge with the
early-summer's evening
(that came sooner to
MacPherson's orchard):
four boys reaching up
for green cheeks peeking down,
and somehow their sourness
was more sweet because
"crazy-man" Jake would
come crashing any second
thru the burdocks to
boot us in the ass,
and once the dog
cornered us and we
clung together low against
the fence and the barbed wire
night sticking to our jeans
and God!   the sweetness
of those apples went
sailing down thru
our terror to the
tips of our
young cocks rising
and crowing to the moon.

# Bloodlines or You Never Can Tell
*For Ian Underhill on the occasion of his retirement
from teaching, June 1996*

How well you've shouldered the burden
of your doubly-dubbed bloodline:
Sir John A. and the reverend-chief Joseph B.
What an exotic alphabet of beginnings,
what a potent (and potentially comic)
gyration of genes to dither
down the unsuspecting generations:

one: a Glaswegian tippler –
his bones a-throb with the rage
of Rob Roy and Culloden –
settled for law and Ottawa,
and hanged the first rebel he saw
though every mutt in Quebec yowl

the other: Iroquoian and
warrior – his blood-brethren could
comb the loams of Onondaga
and finger the faces of the ancients,
his shamans kibitz with Wiskakedjak –
this Mohawk lord who opted for God
and Brantford.

And what, pray, does any such cross-
bred composting portend?
A propensity to sherry, perhaps,
or prinked hairdos?
You never can tell with chromosomes:
they may be no more imposing
than the yarns we swap
in the gloam of Friday-afternoon pubs
to solemnize our sanity.

What matters to us who know you
is not pomp of pedigree or lustre of lineage
but the man you've consented to be:

a pied piper of poems
among the country's young
inkling them to jitter-waltz
in the Wurlitzer of words,
a husbander of those tropes
a nation re-exacts
when mere facts falter,
a plain-talking Scottish
schoolmaster – with Trickster's
        inwit.

But I will see you always:
moccasin-stalking a fairway,
wheedling the convivial rough or
dead-reckoning the rhetoric
of a putt so true
you could build a friendship
        on it.

## Possession

*For Kevin, almost two*

"I-got-it!" you shout:
a single-minded, all-
purpose joy-sound
you clamp on un-
suspecting objects,
laggard adults,
any toy that rhymes
with mine! (or doesn't),
a wee-syllabled
fist-of-a-phrase
you wield like a clout/
ripple like a giggle
to seize the gist of what-
ever in a pounce of
        possession.

And who are we to suggest
that words are merely words
a-jounce in the set-vise
of subject and predicate,
that you do not aver the world
with swaggering surprise/
with the belly-and-bone
pummel of a proto-poem?
(you do, and dare us to doubt)

# Airborne

*For my grandsons sledding
at Doidge Park*

With the glee of gladiators
home-freed from gravity's
boding, you fling your blood-
warm toboggan-bodies
headlong down the wind-
swifted slope, finesse
the sled's eccentric
velocities, and air
borne breathless embrace
the serene absurdity of
not being you or any
other earth-crippled
        Icarus.

Then: the feather-gentled
hiccup of the hill's bottom
arrives you: stilled, un-
singed & glad to be back
in Rome.

## On Watching Tom Play Rugby

*For my grandson, Tom*

It's a game rooted in English rugger
and ball-hog in back alleys,
in Blind Man's Buff and King
of the Castle everywhere, its
intricacies played on a pitch
wider than a Medieval meadow,
greener than graveyard grass.

These boy-battalions clutch
the pigskin as if it were holier
than the Grail herself: Galahads
needing no buckler to blunt
the kamikaze collisions /
tackles abrupt as bone, but
oh the brute beauty of those
sidewinding sprints, the ball
spun outward like a bauble
on Milady's necklace, and that
deft-footed dribble just
leeward of the upright....

Come then the scrum: rivals-all
petrified in a group-hug,
a stone tableau of arrested
body-blows, a centipede's
grip of grunt-and-quake
you might mistake for a Mummer's
dance or Ring-around-a-Rosy,
before the grid unlinks and the ruck
resumes
        and the ancient mayhem
is stinted at last by a handshake.

## Autumn

Autumn was evenings of hide-
and-go-seek under Mara's street-
lamp: oh, how we tendered
ourselves to be flung darkward
by the hundred-thump on the home-post-
beanstalk boys and lope-
leggèd Rapunzels giddy
to be harrowed and hunted by IT
(our Grendel at the castle-gate,
extinction a handspan away).

Pursued, we huddle, gal and guy,
in gendered hollow or neutral
gulch – where something sinister-sweet
croons to my cowpoke courage,
murmurs of mulch where thighs meet
and curves yearn for completion:
        swung between tempt and terror,
        I wait for the "all-free" siren-
        sigh, and masturbate at the moon.

# Effie

Three-year-old Effie: crushed
beneath a two-ton truck, not a block
from the yard where, unaware, I played,
though the shock shook the village for days
and days (and her father till the whiskey
stunned it). Still, at ten, I knew of
death only as a way of ending
stories or the dark shadow stalking
my dreams; but what did elfin Effie
know of it, or for that matter,
what could she surmise of life itself
except as a moment when she was
dancing on the tarmac, and then
to her surprise
                      wasn't?

# The Catch

*For Marg, in loving memory*

Still wary of one another
(me: the usurping male,
you: the mother-in-law of
myth and melodrama)
we find ourselves alone
in a flat-bottomed boat
on Percy Lake the day before
our separate summers end.

For the umpteenth time
I arch my jitterbug
towards the skeptical shore
where lunkers lurk mouthing
frogs by the baker's dozen,
while you sit poised and
patient with landing-net
on the bow, where the last
touch of sunlight sweetens
your face, & I damn near
miss the bass's frantic
heart-leap and tug:
but you, laughing, cheer us both
and together we land the
biggest catch of our life.

# Renewal

*On the occasion of a tree-
planting in memory of
John and Margaret Barnett
For Anne*

Gibbons Park is alive
with memorial trees
(tendril'd saplings among
the ancient, knowing oaks)
with baby-fisted buds
they coax the April breezes
by, bob to home-
coming robins, dream
of autumns and summer sky.

In their thriving is all our
hope: we watch them leap
from Spring to sprouting Spring:
remembrance of those we've lost
deep in the root and in the leaf's
perennial reach
      (your love
kept devout in a tree
taller than eternity).

## Companions

*for John*
*and for Jake, in memoriam*

How you must have yearned for the fence-
free Australian ranges
your dingo forebears
cruised, snapping happily
at the heels of collaborating
cattle and maverick
"roos" – while you huddled
abused, brutally penned,
puppy-struck with terrors
no pedigree could assuage.

And then the last-second
improbable rescue,
a pair of unfisted hands
shaped for soothing, not death,
and a voice enlisting trust,
its own need naked as it
begged and promised
perpetual affection….

And oh what Olympian
companions you became:
marathon chum sprinting
kindred on the home-turf,
generous each with his
gratitude, devout in the
wordless words you used
to promulgate your love.

# Heaven

*For James, seeing snow*
*in the schoolyard*

The school-bell bursts
and oh
such a tribal tumbling
of limb and laughter at the
first everywhere-of-snow —
its tongue-lick/
its mitten-sizzle
no scripture can quell.

In the leaven of
effortless air
boys buffet/
girls twirl on their
tuffets and all the
little heathens find
        Heaven

# The Walk

*For John Barnett: 1911-2001*

With what ease your feet find
the mist-lifting verges
of Percy Lake as the sun
teases morning out of tree-
line and waterway and
shouldering rock, you test
the reach of Bruton Creek
with a lad's lope, abound
in the mid-day's light, move
with the slow, instinctual grace
of a roebuck at home
in a beaver-meadow or a she-
bear ambling a berry-
patch, meander the maze
of a woods you've roved and loved
and superintended with shepherd-
sureness all the long years
of your striding alive amongst pine
and tamarack and red-blooded
maple (the bailiwick of leaf
and bark and stalwart root
you mapped with your heart's
eye) – the afternoon greening
the haze on Haliburton's high
Celtic hills ahead:
you do not falter as the going
steepens, let the evening air
exhilarate, set your sights
on the next beckoning peak,
take a last, devout,
seasoned breath – and with a
flick of your bushman's crook
step up
        and out.

## Every Time it Snows

Anne and I taking Tom
tobogganing on Gibbons' hill,
the snow as thick as Galilee's
on that long-ago mystical Eve,
the night-air stinging and still:
Tom riding his "whee" all the
way down to the feathery bottom
before he can feel what fright is,
Anne and I clinging on
to the seven-year old left in us,
vowing to remember this moment
every time it snows
        or Christmas comes.

## Creation

*For Kevin, James and Tim*

We don't need Darwin
to tell us we've come
from apes and cuddlesome
orang-utans akimbo
on bamboo branches,
the proof is right here
on the schoolyard monkey-
bars, where you three
play Jungle Jim
with your tailless loops
and limb-light aero-
batics, you'd fly
all the way to Heaven
if you had feathers, and dare
the gods of this world
to deny Creation.

# Labour

*For my father, putting a
fieldstone front on our house*

My father once borrowed
a stoneboat to haul
fieldstones (too rooted
to be purged by our fore-
bears) all the way to the
house he'd built for us block
by cinder block: "It needs
a little something to set it off,"
he grinned. I see him still:
a bronzed bareback
Centurion with sledge-
heavy hands cracking
open rocks as hoary
as dinosaur eggs, then
rearing back, wordless,
to savour the prismed
rivulets and pied hues
his body-blow exposed,
now tucking a single
shard into its necessary
niche with an eye as sure
as Michelangelo's; Dad's
mosaic: a brute beauty
hammered out by a
pure labour.

# Patsy: The Silence

*(For Patsy Cline, in memory)*

For you a song was not a thing
to be bruised musical,
gourmandized in the gritty
serenade you served
your worshippers nightly.

For you a song was not the soul's
hungering to be unorphaned
in winged epiphanies
or the appetite for applause.

For you a song was something
shadowed and intricately under:
a lyric air in the brassy sax,
for example, or something
serenely sexed and renegade
in the belly of the brain
and avid for any exit.

You lived your life that way,
each song, crooned and sirened
in the blue laser of fame,
was only halfway yours, a reaching
beyond for what's been lost
already before belonging.
Until the day you took the sky
for breath/surrogate lung,
your lover's grip upon the Cessna's
throttle, you aimed a tender wing
against the sheerest perpendicular,
O you hammered brass/tongued flesh/
the tuning-bone in your throat
upon the effortless air, you
drank the carnivore cry
        of your own death.

While we: merely alive, condemned to endure
(against the taciturnities of time)
the silence of all the songs you'll never sing.

## Good Measure

I am merman

with my one
eyed fin
is all
       swim

in the well
come water

And what purpose
O smooth-skinned
porpoise who are
all heart
beating up
       channel?

I seek the
sea-home
Odysseus al-
most missed

Penelope is
no prize, seaman,
even for your
size

She's the
womb of man –
woman – the sea-
sons reproduce

Circe, you mean
who sang for her supper
(cutlets, I think)
on her poisoned littoral

What are you serving,
        sailor?

I offer up
my eye
like Oedipus

Like Lucifer
catching Eve
in the raw

…in the dappled after-
math I deny
all pleasure

So do I,
but for good measure
I'm keeping
        the apple

# Sketching Anne
*(Christmas morning, 1982)*

If I were to draw you
in lines more loving than words,
they would be Varley's
quickened curves
sketching the essence of
girl in the raw
morning's moment
after love.

But then I
am no Varley, and you
no longer a girl
to be the essence
        of

Take heart,
draw me closer:
it's time we measured
these ageing pleasures
without rhyme.

# To A Daughter, Writing
*Her First Poem*

Twice nine months
we waited for the
word to stir, ravel,
utter itself to
        air:
the first gospel
from that little body's
acrobatic syllabics
we worshipped
            with listening.

For a time, though,
you were content
with the coupling chime
of somersault and the
whees of joy your breath
gave back in rhyme,
we held our own
in awe, in hope
as you flipped dactyls,
spun gymnastic
letters of love
to the everywhere
            around

you mailed your circular
sonnets to yourself
and we loved you
loving them.

At twelve, you stilled:
the will-to-meaning
shamed to silence,
the flesh clenched
on the unutterable
comprehending no
lyric of girlhood
could assuage.

Then: pen on the
precipice of the page –
scapular, scourging,
blood-propelled,
you grip the leveraging
trapeze of a poem
and aim your self
beyond to be, now
                  or ever

## Tom's Song

*(For my grandson, at 18 months)*

Out of the ribbed cradle you croon
the alphabet of your becoming,
each syllable you bend celibate
and cadenced out of your boy's
being once and now
(singsong, rhyme-wild, zany
as the moon's cow)
then unrehearse yourself again
just for the joy of/a newness of
the morning's blue breath
that wafts it wingless
against my ageing ear

I let it soar orphaned
into the resident dream:

full of Afghans
scorched in their crib
and Ethiopian bloat
and lullabies detongued
among the world's rubble

I wake wide with my poet's eye
I crave rage
I beg the absent gods
to let me go loon-mad,
like Tom's song I long just once
to be what I un-am
before the all-anger blooms unassuaged
in the bent fury of the word.

## Say Uncle
*(For my uncle, Bob Gutteridge, on the occasion of his 65th birthday)*

### I

In a wartime village
starved of fathers and
teeming with kids' need
for gun-hipped heroes
to harvest their boy-bravery,
you were the elder
surrogate brother,
the cowboy-commando
who never said uncle.

O how we cheered
your home-run waltz,
your swagger on rink-
quickened blades,
your quarterback's stutterstep
outwitting our clumsy
capture in every scene
that ended in your imp's grin,
the conspirator's wink
we took as adulterous blessing
as the rapture of inclusion
in the game about-to-be-played
somewhere just beyond the
fission of sky and
blood-linked sun.
And so we mimicked
and marched and mimed
your hungering and fed
our enthusiasm for oblivion
and happy endings –
till the day you rode
wilfully into the sunset
(where baby-faced snipers
grieve in the cinematic dark)

## 2

Wars cease, heroes come back
to famished applause,
I grew tall, oddly
ordinary, but you
(imp's laugh scotched,
abaft) had the courtesy
to remain avuncular,
as big as the dream-uncle
in my grandson's blue eye.

Somehow
you kept the "kid-in-you"
intact, beyond age or
the sniper's felicity,
and even now (65 and
grateful for the years
that numb and cauterize)
you pass it generously
down the generations
of nephews and childhood lore:
it is the cause,
the hope you fought for.

## 3

May you prosper
here among those you love
and there
amid the vast village
of stars and fostering suns.

# Home

## 1

This season hillbilly is
camp, quaint as
Granny's damson jam,
it suits our city passion
for matters country and
local, exotic and
downhome-ish

Yesteryear you all
were bug-eyed idiots
slouched with shotgun
(or peasant-breasted)
grinning your peculiar
untouchable malice
outward at silly tourists
lost in the maze
of interbred back-
woodsy lanes.

## 2

Only your music
tells the whole
story, it cannot lie
even when it wants to,
there's no disguise
for truth in the
corruptive twanging and
nasal sentimentalities
we have appropriated
with virtuous civility –

the voice within
the singing within
the singer reaches
        thru
and makes us listen
as if song herself
were the eldest muse
on earth
        and new

And you, Loretta,
make memorable
again your own
ancestral earthsong:
the skirl of Celtic
rage in Boadicea's
cry, her valleys
ravaged by Tuscan
campmongers, the
glee-wail of
Irish fife in the
muffling green glens,
the harp in Arthur's halls
condensing heaven in the
wake of Saxon drums,
the tom-tom's muted
lament for the lost
forever Cherokee hills,
the fiddle's hopscotch
skipping-rope dance
on your father's hand-
made floorboards, a
mother's timeless lullabies
filling the only room
any of us can ever
        call home.

# Alphabets

*For Loretta Lynn*

## I

Once more I watch
the film that tries to
free you from cliché,
pin down the essential
myth, make you more
and less than you were,
and somehow misses the
point

        you

were more than a
country balladeer
anthologizing your
father's lost eyes
no song could assuage
with its ersatz hope and
public good-cheer so
prized in the bistros
you praise and deny.

And less than a
daughter-of-the-dialect
savagely noble in her
hollows and coombes
untinctured by time
or the brutal sloughs
of suburb and alley:
the Hollywood dream
of our death's flesh
resurrected in the
random blue crocus,
the green incarnation
of the local.

**2**

You were and are
simply yourself,
surprised by the songs
that spring like iambic
from a bard's tongue,
stunned by their
wonder, by the flawed
marble of their
making in the
sweet/hurt/lost/loving
crucible no
words can touch
with their tremor.

Though I try —
because you too
are one of the poets
doomed by lot
to probe with a
ferret's stare
the foetal dens
where earth's urgings
fester, and blazon
the alphabets of poetry
                and despair.

## Soliloquy, For Lovers

*(For my mother and father, in memoriam)*

**1**

Come with me, our paired blades
snare cadence, the ice
horizonless: we will dare passage

I am scared: of the free-fall ice
lends, of freedom and bondage

Once I skated alone to the village-edge
beyond the eave of the last shanty
over marsh-ice the moon's
elemental glow reduced to diamond
these skates shredded in frenzy,
I tell you there was no pivot-point
but the carbon-dark of my breathing

I saw you first, gladiatorial, teething
on cheers, you couldn't guess my need
for grace in the nub of violence, blood
on your brow stirs in me
something retrieved from summer

The cheers surround me, urge surrender,
like a village they would take possession
with applause – I open flesh
with a stick, its blood is green:
I will not show cause

They see the act, male and outlaw,
I recognize the deed, the girl
shyness in the shape of your skating,
lust propelling every dance
we disguise it from, after all
I wound the ground I walk on

I saw you first, an eye stalking me,
estranged; your voice orphan,
your plaudit predatory, yet something
akin to winter in it, the victor
fox made victim by the cold

Let ours be a summer-love, propelled
by the winters that close it in

Let ours be a winter-love, mocked
by the summers that shut it out

## 2

I never dreamt a February courting,
the moon passionate in black,
snow lush against sill and eave,
trees amnesiac over burrows
our bodies forge with their warmth:
love, like the village driven
inward to the pivot-point,
is lit with its own element

I am stunned by gentleness,
yours and my own, the ice
on the shanty walls entrances –
the lake mocks us with its miles,
I want to skate its distance
to death, take you utterly
into aloneness, make us both
orphans in a new world

I have that part of you curled
inside me, the eaves are breathing

I am afraid of your ease,
of freedom and bondage

I love you
I will not hold it hostage

I love you
I give you this village

Let us believe the future

Let us share passage

Let the dance be mutual

# The Innocents

*For Loretta Lynn*

## 1

Against the grate
of G-major, your
notes take flight
like birdsong at the
birth of light
no day can measure

Melody held
between wing and the
wing's wedging
of air, you sail
the sky's endless
edge against
        gravity

## 2

Such innocence
cannot be borrowed
and set to lyric ends,
cannot be lent
or feigned (alas)
to mend with music
those sorrows we
open to it in
perpetual expectation

It is the gift
of song itself,
of singing
in the singer

Nor does it bring us
the sweet unclutter
of Eden's engendering,
the child's unsubtle
seeing we all
pretend to love
or regret the passing of —

The innocence I hear is
dark with the knowledge
of what has been lost/
forgotten/surrendered
to sentiment or art,

but oh, your voice
carries its terrible news
high and sweet and tender
into the uncompromising sky
our secret hearts
reach out to ....

# 3

You were born
one of those few
lyric choristers who
bore witness to
earth's breech-birth, the
first leaching of light,
who saw and sang and
made remembrance
        your vow:

the lark, homeless
in his meadow
transfiguring pain
into panegyric

the robin, alone
at dawn
murmuring her pro-
and epithalamion

## Abelard's Plea

Headache again?

No, the nunnery

I have grown to love
the chaste walls
I look upon
with impunity,
the snowdrops un-
visited by bees,
the tufted greenery
of my June garden,
the fresh light
along these sills
to see the world by

It was so good
last time, you do
remember, don't you?

Too long between letters –
the summers you confected
with words, tropes, the
rhythms imprisoned
in your cleft flesh
I caught with my
virgin's blood, turned
inward to spring
outward to hope

or the winters you etched
with trochee, iambic,
metaphors of despair
that made me somehow
whisper
spero
sperandum est

What do you think
I am, a eunuch?

No never that

For years I husbanded
the joy of our first union,
nursed it with a child's
wild hunger till it
grew eloquent
in its own light

Something I said, then?

Yes, and not said
I need symbols, gestures,
verbs in the future tense,
nouns to sharpen the
distance between us,
unleash the seasons
to pain and poetry

I love you
I love you

Not enough

I'm sitting upright
in the cloistered light

Upon the intact
wall of my memory
I scratch with this
crooked crayon
the first
        blood-budding
        obscenity

# Afterimage
*(For Anne)*

No lover's eye
could cope with the
girl in the Volkswagen's
sigh against the curb:

a wince of
lemon dress,
red hair
piled high,
flesh pebbled with
mother-of-pearl and a
smile hinting
hope in the
        May sky

(but I try)

"Hi," you say,
"It's time we flew!"

And we do

# Heart: 1944

We zigzagged Blind
Man's Buff on the staggered
steps of the Monument
to the Great War's dead
at the still centre of the village,
unaware in our ragtag
manoeuvres that our fathers' names
might well be etched some
day in cold strokes
upon that sheer pillar
and the unmarked soldier
shouldering the sky, and we
paused just long enough
in the rough-and-tumble
of our upstart games
to hear the stone beat
of its granite heart.

## Bones

*For grandfathers everywhere*

Our bones age slowly
but surely towards the dark
December of our years...
I think of my own grand-
father in his Saturday
morning workshop
(snug in an embering heat)
those callused hands
making the lathe sing,
while outside the wind
yearns and Winter
hungers after Spring.

# Hands

*For my father, dying young*

Always I see your hands
rough upon hammer
and chisel, brace and bit,
working wonders with wood,
the home you built for us
brick and mortar and grace
of line levelled with the eye
of a lithographer, I loved
the way your fingers fuelled
the urge propelling them
as they fashioned the pelts
of foxes and big-horn
sheep into elegant
friezes, the way they strummed
a ukulele you hummed
the latest hit to, their warrior's
grip on a hockey stick –
a man of prodigious talents
but not one of them
could save you, nor all
my worshipping of those rough,
wood-weary hands.

# First Steps

*For Katie-Ann*

Your toes tingle the broad
pool of air and a leg
steps strident into its
smooth immensity,
the body follows with a feel
of floating,
      then you grin
to let us know it's okay
to applaud.

# Routine

*For my grandfather*

They called you a creature
of habit, cycling home
each day at precisely
five minutes to five,
not a jot more or less,
standing before your evening
lathe watching the bit
shave its steadfast shapes,
abed by ten, up by six,
lover of everything ordinary.
Perhaps they didn't know
about the chaos of war,
the blood-drenched trenches,
the stunning staccato of guns,
the screams of the near-alive,
the shell that halved your hip,
your fear unforgiven –
all that would have made
a leisurely bike-ride
after a seamless day's work
feel like Heaven.

# Poet

The poet as philanderer
weds words to one another,
then without a may-I or please
commits adulterous anarchies.

The poet as cartographer
maps emotion with metaphor,
then without a wink or give-a-damn
makes mazes of Meridian.

The poet as your parson
catechizes the lexicon,
then without a by-your-leave or a nod
blames the meaning on God.

# Malamute in Snow

*For Annie*

At the first sniff of snow
she paws the air with both
nostrils as if it were ripe
with pheromones – impelled
by some homing instinct
as antic as her malamute
genes, by some Arctic urge
remembered in the blood,
by some longing to be albino:
she does a muktuk dance
in the huddled drifts,
a whirligig in the blizzard's
might, she embraces the trans-
mutated landscape
as if she were elemental with it –
they blur as one in a last
whiff of white.

# So Big

*For Anne and Katie-Ann*

"So big!" you croon,
lifting the little one
fingertip high –
the giggle begins in your toes,
thrums on the taut tummy,
and follows her eyes moon-
ward.
      Oh the pure
innocuous pleasure
of embodied sensation,
the mingling of two smiles
across the generations.

# God-Spell
*For Marybelle Cooper*

I worshipped you from afar,
that is across the pickets
between our house and Cooper's,
the morning sun haloed
in your hair, those brand-new
breasts purring in plaid,
for you I would be Galahad
on a white-hot charger,
Lancelot bringing back
tokens of super devotion,
I would be Lord of the Rings,
St George and his dragon-foe –
till you smiled, said "hello,"
and the god-spell was broken.

## April

Like a loose machine-gun
your rat-a-tat-tat
spices the neighbourhood,
the insurgent love-song
of the red-bellied woodpecker
(with a jackhammer chorus),
you put out the drum-roll
call to any willing female,
a lonesome lover
enthused with April urges.

# Nouns

*For Katie-Ann at one year*

## 1

You sit surrounded by
objects that have no name,
free to be tasted and touched,
they spin in your sight as big
as balloons unanchored
by language, while we frantically
feed you noun after noun,
coaxing syllables out of the
giddy twists of your tongue
till word-and-thing are wedded
one in wonder.

## 2

Nouns are the first to come
and the first to go – they
vanish one by one from the
bright page of our memory
till there's nothing left to say
but white.

# Boyhood

*For Bobby Cooper*

Under high summer skies
Bobby and I a-bob
the whale-blue lake,
dolphin-wise we plunge
and spout like twinned trout,
mirror one another's
movements in coy
unison, scan
the dunes for pirates
and lost legionnaires,
sun ourselves side
by side on the thigh-warm
sands of Canatara.

Later, in the
darkening change-room
we compare shy
erections and swear
blood-oaths to the joys
of boyhood
        forever.

# Immanence

*For Anne, Kate and Tom*
*Christmas, 1990*

Somewhere snow is always
falling like this: all
singing succinct within
all silence outward its bliss —
no birth-trumpeting here
of Christ's arousal
in Bible-bloodied flesh,
no hallelujah wind-hymn
bassooning fold and hummock
and star-bitten crèche,
no earthy carolling
of artful joy to
deafen the world
of hope and hearkening
in the heretic heart,
no holy-ghosting quartet
to roundelay with
        dutiful Death

just snow
that is always somewhere
rising
        like this
        oh

gentling white
dwarf's zero-breath
(bone blizzard, un-
mangered flesh)

Our Lord's
sigh of surprise.

# The Absolute Uncertainty of Being Seven

*For Tom on his 7th Birthday*

**1**

We do not ask to
be at any age,
flung once we are
by some muscle-
flinching mother-
womb airward
to light's oblivion
and the gravity-ache
of bone-breath in the
absolute suddenness
of flesh and
        aspiration.

## 2

You did not ask to be
seven, but you are —
these birthday balloons
grinning adultly and
numinously numbered
say so, and you are
too loving to demur,
to admit what all
the womb-born carry
aching in them:

the certainty that
bones don't gravitate
and a day is a
        day
to be lit with
        absolute breath.

# Moment
*For Tim, laughing*

## 1

The manic marionette
in the music box
croons to baby-Tim
Send in the clowns
Where are the clowns?
its lullaby bubble-
notes trapezing
out of odd elbow
or string-loose
percussive knee:
a puppetry of
unbedighted
        delight,

we muse, goo-
going prompts
till what irrupts
just for us
is an indigestive
lip-mimetic
        pucker.

"He smiled!" we clap
in grandparental glee,
"Come see!"
But Tim peers
otherwise: pristine
eyes colloquize
Mr. Punchinello's
gigantic lyric-
strummed calico
        antics,
and a polkadot
giggle dazzles
down pink-
skinned and blood-
flush to infant
ivory-bones
humming their own
        harmonic.


## 2

Chastened by joy
we listen askew,
attend to the
clownness of things
musical
        and
           momentous.

# Walking

*For Anne, on her birthday*
*June 10, 1993*

You took me walking
upon Doon Pinnacle
to show me the stars
you loved from afar,
their touch luminous
in the grass we brush
barefoot in our passing.

You took me walking
on your father's farm
to show me the pastures
of your girlhood gone:
its home-hills,
barns bereft,
hearthstones
fragile as ash,
daisies in a field
once drowsy with horses
where lovers doze
in their dream-flesh

You took me walking
down Avenue Road
to show me the city
you chose for romance
and rite of passage,
whose torch-tune was a
jazz appassionata
to a moon operatic
in its urges, and O
under it June
women promenade
in their urban bones.

You took me walking
among star-tipped hills
wildflower meadows
the boulevards of town –
and we found such
pleasure in
moving together
we took our walking
by the hand

and kept it going.

# A Word to
# My Grandsons

*For my grandfather*

Even now, across the
no-man's-land
of your sudden goodbye
in the midst of my own
too-eager arrival,
your grandfather-voice
rings as true as the
stories you told me
teetered on the precipice
of three and perched heroic
on the aerie promontory
of your knee, the soothsaying
body-beat of your heart
a simple breath away,

You let me be the
brick-quick pig,
the gruffest billy-
beast, the huntsman
with the wolfbane/hood-
winking gun, or (when
the ground wavered under
the wind-cliffs of my reach)
Goldilocks dream-
snug in her purloined
bed, Cinderella
rapturing princes and
pliant pumpkins
for ever and after,

you let me stare straight
at the sun as your brows
knit lupine, lips
a-quiver for anything
caped and carnal,
the pullet's scream you
fabulate before Brer
Fox bites down on
death and foolish plots,
and when I turn for a
last loving look —
you are grandfather again,
all your tropes gentle
as parentheses, your soldier's
smile a salute and a kind
of forgiving, even then
you tried to craft the
tale exact, to ape
familiar the voices
of chastening girlhood
and wizened wolf-
wink, of trolls a-cry
in drowned kingdoms
and gloating boy-goats,
of princesses too blond
for their own good and
parlour-maids humble
enough to be struck
pure by dumb luck,

and never once letting me
in on the secret you thought
I'd captured in my delight
and precipitate plunge:
that ogre-croak
and king-whistle
and the avuncular hug
of words in our room
were never ours to hoard
or hone, but borrowed
only and harp-rung
from hearth-to heart

(as now I know
       and do).

# Vivacity

*For Claire Organ
on her 40th birthday*

## 1

Your grin would make a pixy
blush with comparison
and bend her back-
words hopscotch jig
to another's praise,

nor will "elfin" quite do
to catch the puckish
acrobatics your eyes
deploy to keep the
world off-stride and
sweeten its severities.

Your skeptic's guffaw
would make a bull
moose yaw and
notice the moon-
embossed stars a slim
inch above his nose.

So we too are
freed through you
to leaven our commonplace
lunacies with laughter
and neighbourly
        complicity

## 2

Such vivacity
does not evolve
in Darwinian degrees
nor is it wholly
bestowed by the
fertile nurture of
home-and-hearth-
bred seasons
(it mocks the very
years and birthdates
we concoct to confirm
its having been)

Such joy unscheduled
just arrives and is –
you brought it with you
blood-and-baby-
boned bobsledding
your way into being:
you tasted May's day
once / wondered
at the etch of
        breath
upon a dawn
frosted with bobolinks
and meadow-welcome –

you laughed,
        and were.

You smile,
        and are.

# Wheels

*For Greg Curnoe, 1936-1992*
*In Memoriam*
*[Greg Curnoe was killed in a*
*cycling accident five days*
*before his 56th birthday, and*
*one week before the opening*
*in Toronto of his most recent*
*work: a series of self-portraits]*

A wheel is the
quintessential region
wefting us countywise
thru Middlesex concessions/
the Queen's highroad/
townlines strict
as Simcoe's sextant,
giving way in the gloam
of our consensual pedalling
to forked riverruns
wooded with elfenwelsh,
a moccasined apse
meandering as an
Attawandaron's dream,
and something instinct
in the hillock's heart-
beat egging us on
beyond the range of
ordinary light
to infinite peripheries
whose cooling suns
splinter spectrally and
blow bugle-orange
and exuberant blue.

Or: wheeling us art-
fully innerward
with spun spokes in
shimmering symmetries
diminished to the dot-
hypnotic at the ego-hub –
its humming basic
as a daub / a breath-stroke
the home-colour of your
quixotic painter's eye
inking the
        Earth ...

... with portraits of jazz
pianos, kazoos tuned
to a chaos catapulting
chrome yellows and spasmic
purple thru the landscape
of acquaintance and wit-
tinted humoresque
where pals dubbed Jack
or Hugh or Exley consort
in alphabetical dis-
order, or tundras
untouchably far
stilled in acute
expectancy by the
primary prism: your love
for hearthground, the seasons
of genealogy, maps
primordial or wistfully
palimpsest, for a

country of counties
(crayoned by schoolkids
imperfect in their ease),
for the tug of neighbourhood,
for Sheila limned
with effortless affection,
for the ultimate orbit
of images (Greg glancing)
we seize to steady our
grief / our slim grip upon
the Catherine-wheel that ferried
you
        vanishing
        from us.

# Necessities

*For Bill Exley, vocalist with the Nihilist Spasm Band,
and in memory of Greg Curnoe.*

## 1

Like some freak-
show pitchman
barking beatitudes,
or epicene Gabriel
hell-bent for a toot,
or a raging New Age
Cassandra in drag –
you shimmy and hoot
your no-news gospel,
bray its naysaying
doomsday welcome
like Lucifer's donkey
with a bull-horn in its snout
(rebuttal in each
quixotic twitch)
while all around you the
hand-hewn tenderly
tinted instruments
of pandemonium
cry dissonance
to the gut-bucketing
serenade of the double-
negative funnelled
up thru the fret and
strum of your prisming

bones to absolute
zero at the lip: you howl
like Hamlet's stand-in
disenvowelled:

NO CA - NA - DA - DA - DA !

(and other necessary
        nihilisms).

## 2

And yet, for all this
impastoral racket —
every un-gesture
of your non-song is
parody, is pale
mimesis of
something already
sung and assumed:

Louis Armstrong,
for example, blowing
blues thru a warped
kazoo, Guy Lombardo
on "uppers" smokin'
a New Year's rag,
Glen Miller gone

nude in-the-mood,
trumpet tom —
fooleries from Mugsy
or Bix, the Beatles in
ball-gowns wafting
sweet nadas to Mick
and the crew tarted up
in pink tuxedos…

And each glandular
beep or dinning to
drown Beethoven in
decibels / Mozart
in mayhem, to dis-
connect the rock
from roll, hobble
the jig of jazz —
is but to play
the common madcap
        idiom
(impishly improvised)

And every Dada-derly
plink of denial
reminds us simply
of the note it is
        not,
that music (like our lives)
is more echo than artifice,
and of that anguish loud
(of loss/of grief) not even
the null-drum of
        oblivion
can obliterate

(But still —
the mouth with the mega-
phone persists:
simpers obscenities,
tongues its word —
turbulence in the
spectrum-spill of
joyful noise
you and Beelzebub's
bandsmen are bound
to soliloquize
in dissolute
        communion).

# 3

And more than this:
your loud-hailing de-
syllabifications, your
Jacobean hyperbolic,
your palindromes of mock –
poetic disabuse
no one – least of all
Lear's fool, Hamlet's
antic, or the nay-singer
himself whose quarter-tones
gong as orotund
as Prospero's iambic,
whose god's-eye is as
hectic as Miranda's
(islanded/innocent)
hearing on high
the Book of the World –
and refusing
        to accept it.

# Where the Voice Abides

*For k.d. lang, in concert at*
*Lulu's Roadhouse, March 15, 1990*

## 1

Even the letters
of your billboard
fame have been shrunk
to match the shyness
of a prairie smile under
miles of androgynous
sky — so, too,
the hand-me-down
look of improbable
patch-and-flair, that
tufted jut of hair:
its neuter, abbreviate
vee — raw amid such
engendering

    BUT


dwarfed on a vast
vacancy of stage
you become some hamlet
from southern Alberta
crouched in a
howl of sun, drowned
by light from the
seasonless winds, and
fearing such freedoms
you give us no sign

      AS

the band behind you
roars its welcome,
O ersatz rockabilly-suite
of jazzed piano, percussed
guitar, the eclectic
lick of fiddle and
bass – insatiable drum
of what we've come for

      BUT

still you demur,
swaddled in flood-lit
mother-warmth and the
opium of applause,
you seem to fold
inward on some girl's
hurt –

and give us no warning

      AS

you are everywhere
strung: warp-and-
woofer / electric
hyperbole for the
tribal tongue

## BUT

still you feign to
play the wallflower:
ducking mirrors, the
sight of what might be un-
petalled in vee
      or tuck,
and fearing such freedom
you offer no token
no hope of where
the voice comes from.

## 2

The voice arrives
sudden as sin
big-boned and quick
with surprise – mega
sexed and earthy as
Ella or Kitt or
Piaf on a bender, as
Bessie-on-booze all
sweated with love's
disgust, as Callas
ripping at the doll's
crib of her life,
as Patsy riding
the lyric horn
        down…

                        BUT

here your pelvic
flute sweetens
the ozone ear,
opens it up to the
yin-and-yang of
juiced blues and
Cajun twang, of
rose-hipped western
swing at the country
gate – (the treble-touch
of a girl-boy body
just stung by the
anguish of song)

## AND

here on this prairie-siding stage
with your little-lettered Alberta name
astride your own organ
voice – you face all
the freedoms for us:

and we forgive you
with shameless applause

## BUT

you give nothing away
not even to yourself –
though I like to think
you would have joined us, as
in our stunned repose
we begin to surmise
the home-zone
where the voice abides.

# Stories

*For Ferguson Jenkins, on his entering
baseball's Hall of Fame, July 21, 1991*

## 1

They trace your career
with the clean trajectory of
one of your 10,000 curves,
with digital winningness
across The Nation's screens,
another inning in the
North American dream –
play: black boy
so white with talent
even the yokels of that
backwater "burg" in a
cold hockey-country
(where John Brown, once,
conspired and fraternized)
could not miss the
Hall-of-Fame hum
in the rookie zeal
that took you down
to the redneck circuits
where you surmounted
loneliness, a sapling
slider, the casual
bigotry no father's
counsel could gentle
        away
then on to The Show,
knight-errant with the
archer's arm smack
in the middle of
Mister Wrigley's pure
palace of pitch-and-hit,
O green sward and
English ivy on the

folk-stone wall to
keep all our illusions
sun-lit and centred
on the dark-skinned
paladin from Chatham, Ont.
bucking history and
statistics and the
urchin gods of chance
and the hapless Cubs –
till here you stand
podium-tall at
Cooperstown: public
agent for your race,
its prize in your
      pitcher's fist.

## 2

But there's more than
one kind of story,
for example: Saturday
morning fathers-and-sons
angling the genteel Thames
 or playing catch and pepper
till the moon chafed,
and there is the simple
love-of-the-game
sustained beyond
the wins and losses,
the dead-end finishes,
the roster of
sluggers dethroned –
it takes a humble

kind of courage
to throw a hundred pitches
day-in-and-side-out,
the salient hunger
in The Batter's eye,
the mound your only
toehold as diamonds/stadia/
glittering cities/the
migrant stars spin
on the axis of your arm
you rise to throw
a hundred pitches and
each as good as the
one dreamt of that day
a father's nod
told you which
story you could become:

fastball crooning
in its low zone,
curves with a bend
obedient as bamboo
in a fisherman's grip,
your slider lithe in the
hitter's gape, then
                            lethal

and spring-by-summer
the seasons pass and
hope in its guises
and still you rise to
throw your hundred pitches
the mound a steady
home beneath you
and the years bring
birth and sorrow and
small betrayals and
still the curves and

sliders number in the
hundreds and rarely a
cliché amongst them
and love fails as it
must while death thrives
(you mourn a mother's
passage from one
darkness to another
more welcoming)
and still the day
demands its hundred
pitches (your curve
no longer willow,
the low hummer sings
occasionally in the
ivied twilight) and
mindful of all
your recent griefs –
in the gloaming of that
ancient everyman's arena –
you pitch to such
aplomb not one
of A Nation's bigots
notices the colour
of your perfection

(you who have known
with a heart braver
than itself that love's
parable is best:
your proud blind
mother fingering the
seams on her boy's
smile).

# Mother

*For Kate and Tim*

## 1

First the throbbing
sea-broth thickens
to brutal black
in the all-surround
the rhythmic, womb-
stroke panics, flesh-
combs cringe as
something not-you
unswaddles itself,
its skin-scream
soundless all the
slithering blood-
tunnelled way down:

you are the thing
expunged,
a cry to stun
the dismembered air,
a last grope
for the cut cord,
the blast of
umbilical-breaking
light.

## 2

No wonder, then,
battened on this
sudden breast,
you attach lip
to ruptured nozzle,
suck lungward,
ache for the
honey-drum
of a heartbeat
      remembered.

**3**

Flesh-drowsed, bone –
content, lapped
by some convenient
foetal-curved
limb that clings
you homeward to
       sleep,
you are startled
by the presence of
eyes exotic
in the dream-dusk:
buzzing with word –
murmurs that touch
and grieve, and
promise much …

It is then you take
your first look at the
other staring back
accepting what it sees.

**4**

When you wake
she is still there.

## The Time Between

In the time it takes to blink
an eye I can resurrect
my village: its streets
and hectic alleys a Braille
I read with the fingertips
of memory, the faces
of my boon companions
as vivid now as when
I first drew their image
each night before prayers –
Butch and Bones and Wiz –
and, despite the odds, I
will them back again,
as if the time between had never
been and innocence
might outlive our brief
and joyful boyhood.

## Out of the Blue

Out of the blue a call
from a boyhood chum,
his name faintly stirring
at the edge of memory,
and quick as it's recovered
I am back in King
Edward Public School,
the years peeled away
as if they had never been,
and once again I am stunned
by the ease with which the past
obtrudes upon the present,
and nothing is ever lost:
not even the pain of what
we can never fully
regain.

# The Sands of Canatara

We swam so long in the Lake
we grew gills to go with
our fins, and dolphin-eyed
we plied the playful waves,
while the beach beckoned:
the sands of Canatara
stretched like a nubile loop
around the bay,
arrayed with dunes we
commandeered with our sea –
warm bodies, let the
heat of the day-lit
sun anaesthetize
our blood as we lay
elongate in the bone –
white light.

# The Welcoming

*For my grandparents*

For forty years you slept
in the same bed, cocooned
against the intruding world,
embracing the darkness
with your twinned bodies,
your meshed flesh, till one
of you had the audacity to die,
and Gran thereafter
abandoned your mutual
room, left it to its own
emptiness till the day
she too was welcomed
        home.

# The Word

Annie's grown old,
no longer tempted
by moles sprouting from the under
earth of her favourite field,
no longer straining
at the leash and dreaming
of malamutes hauling
sleds over a shimmer
of snow, blood pounding
in her Arctic heart –
Annie's grown old,
peering up through sad
knowing eyes, waiting
for us to say the word.

# It's Hard To Believe
*For Potsy in memoriam*

It's hard to believe you're gone,
you were so filled with life,
you sprang from the womb rambunctious
and looking for someone to try
your sly wit upon,
you gave your mother a run
for her money, you were the big
brother I never had,
taking me to football games
and fishing on Cameron Lake,
you regaled us with story after
story till all the plots
ran out, and you left us
blessing the years we knew you.

In the last year of your life
you start telling stories
of your distant youth:
derring-do from the War,
like the time you huddled
in the belly of a Lancaster,
eighteen years young,
a rifle across your knees,
waiting for the Jerries to come
slinking out of the Irish night:

you weave such tales
in your avuncular voice
as if out of some sudden
deep need to tell
your life before all the stories
abruptly stop – and me
no longer your loving
        listener.

## Me

There before the camera
Mother and Father stand
holding an infant up
for all the world to see
what love has wrought in its first
flush: the child is me
seventy years young,
ready to be sprung
upon the world.

## Love's Seasons

This is the autumn of our love:
gone are the May days
of our courtship, the duo-
dance we did with such vim
and verve, gone too
our summering love
grown deft and wise,
and we are left with September's
lush decline, for us
there will be no winter
for like the fall flower
we shall take a last bow
and flame out.

# The End of Days

When I think of the end
of days, I remember
the village that let me be,
where I hailed each morning
raw with sunshine,
that guided me hazily
through afternoons ripe with
cowpokes and Comanches
on the Prairie below the River
and the Lake ardent as oceans,
where I reconnoitred
the village verges that kept
me safe through the evenings
effortless with hide-
and-go-seek as we spun
the intimate Other
in the Indian-giving
        darkness.

# Sin

*For Tommy Fahselt*

We cared not that Eve
tasted the apple and fed
it happily to Adam,
for the golden orbs that hung
in MacPherson's orchard
were more tempting than
the trees of the Hesperides –
Tommy and I roostering
through forbidden terrain,
gorging on appleflesh
as sweet as sin.

## Wee

What I remember
is grandmother's verandah
shadowed in the summer's
smothering sun, a robin's
throbbing lyric in the wind –
lush leafage, the wee
rush of lethargy
in the hum of our hobbled
        blood.

What I remember
are the thigh-high snows,
icicles teasing the eaves,
the thrill of being swallowed
by something bigger than
ourselves, trembling
the wee blizzard inside
us, the chilled bone
of our being.

# Music
*For Rebecca*

The music box plays
a lilting melody,
your wee body sways
to the tilt and tenor of its tune
as if a musical Muse
inside you rocks
to some song singing
solo in your bones.

# About the Author

**Don Gutteridge** was born in Sarnia in 1937, raised in the nearby village of Point Edward and now lives in London, Ontario. He taught High School English for seven years between 1960 and 1968. In 1968 he became a Professor in the Faculty of Education at Western University, where he is now Professor Emeritus. He is the author of seventy books including: poetry, fiction and scholarly works in educational theory and practice. He has published twenty-two novels, including the twelve-volume Marc Edwards mystery series, and thirty-five books of poetry, one of which, *Coppermine*, was short-listed for the 1973 Governor-General's Award. In 1970 he won the UWO President's Medal for the best periodical poem of that year, "Death at Quebec." To listen to interviews with the author, go to: http://thereandthen.podbean.com.

www.ingramcontent.com/pod-product-compliance
Lightning Source LLC
Chambersburg PA
CBHW020123130526
44591CB00032B/485